ὕβρις
IVRIS

Misha the Maniac

© Michael Alexandratos, 2021

This book is copyright. Apart from any fair dealing for the purposes of study and research, criticism, review, or as otherwise permitted under the Copyright Act, no part may be reproduced by any process without written permission. Inquiries should be made to the publisher.

National Library of Australia
Cataloguing-in-Publications entry
Misha the Maniac,
IVRIS
ISBN: 978-0-6488079-6-4

Book design: Gareth Sion Jenkins
Edited: Josh Mei-Ling Dubrau & Gareth Sion Jenkins

Typeset in Roboto Light: 10pt, 11pt.
Published by Apothecary Archive, January, 2021
www.apothecaryarchive.com

Apothecary Archive operates on Gadigal land.

ὕβρις
|
|

|

IVRIS
|

The cover image is based on the following design taken from a liturgical book in the collection of the Byzantine and Christian Museum in Athens, Greece.

At the top of the design is a royal crown of "temperance" and "self-control" (σωφροσύνη) that triumphs over the sexual vices and sins below.

The root on the bottom translates loosely as "lustfulness", and the stem reads "adulterers and the sexually immoral are judged by God", which is taken from Hebrews 13:4.

The leaves on the right and left of the stem include the sins of masturbation, sodomy, homosexuality, incest, adultery, bestiality and promiscuity.

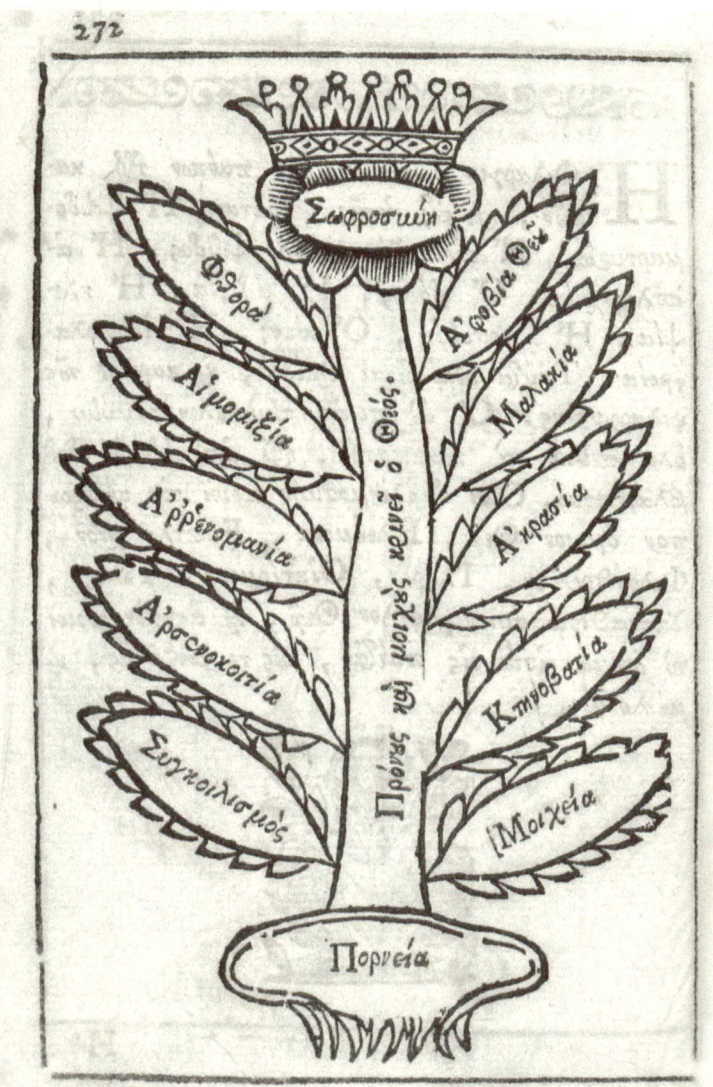

"Aspects of the sin of 'fornication'". Wood-cut from a Heirmologion (liturgical book containing hymns of the Christian Orthodox Church). Venice 1772 (Printhouse of Ioannis Glykis from Ioannina). Permission granted by the BYZANTINE & CHRISTIAN MUSEUM, Athens, Greece (inv. no.: BXM 17703).

The Greeks had a relation to something that they called ὕβρις ... European man, since the beginning of the Middle Ages, has had a relation to something he calls, indiscriminately, Madness, Dementia, insanity ... the σωφροσύνη of the Socratic reasoners owes something to the threat of ὕβρις ... [this] Reason-Madness nexus constitutes for Western culture one of the dimensions of its originality; it already accompanied that culture long before Hieronymus Bosch, and will follow it long after Nietzsche and Artaud.

—Michel Foucault, *Madness and Civilization.*

ὕβρις (ivris) = hubris, pride, insolence.

σωφροσύνη (sofrosini) = temperance, self-control, moderation.

Contents

Breaking Out	13
Hark, Listen!	15
Declaration	16
Word Melt	17
Genesis	19
Faggot Lucifer	20
Septic Tank Universe	22
Flesh to Feed Souls of the Dying	24
Tax Fund Carcass	29
Coins	31
The Apotheosis of Hedwig Wilms at Berlin Buch	32
Babushka	34
Jacob's Dream	36
Try Something New: Porn	38
Natural Causes	39
1453 A.D.	41
Fagia	42
Hedwig Wilms Redux	44
The Holy City	48
Night of Glass	49

Live at the Whisky a Go Go	51
Dodecameron Suite	53
Polka-dot	63
This Could Be Anywhere	64
Konzert	66
Static Bugs	68
Event Scores	71
The End, My Friend	76
Oil Blood Bones Stigmata	77
Corpus	78
EAT THE WORDS	79
Jump Cut	82
Dream Places	83
Dachau Blues	84
Wood of Suicides	85
Death Piece	86
Nausea	87
Discharge Summary	88
The Puppet	95

Breaking Out

Feel the surge of energy. BREAKING OUT. The thought of an animal. BLEAK. ENERGY. POWER. LIGHT. BREAKING OUT. Stooping at the last foothold. TAKE ME NOW. Feeling on the cusp. Breaking through. GO TO HELL!

MYSTERY. WONDER. LOVE. LONELY TEARS.

GOD! GOOD GOD! So close to the fantastic visions of Muhammad the immaculate prophet yet so very FUCKING FAR. PLEASE. I am the train tracks, the train tracks breaking down, slowing down. AGGGGGGHH.

The stop osmosis creature, the finality in light. Stop the bombs. STOP THE BOMBS! Tearjerker force spark. Electrocute me NOW I'm an <u>ANGEL</u> and I am running out of time. Take hold of me and let me DIE.

I am a GOD. I am a VISIONARY. I <u>AM</u> the onerous dream. Death star collapse and retribution. Asinine plastic pieces fucking CRACK.

LET ME DIE!

STOP THE TRACKS!

Cancer is a fucking privilege. Blue bolts in the jellyfish, an anathema of justice programming into mind, and the comatose kittens amazed in the rhapsody of esquire sports. Sports! The brute force! Boys, let me cry and open up the floodgates.

GOD IS DEAD. THE WAR IS OVER. There is nothing in the air but VICTORY!

Jesus take hold of me. Calling far away. Comatose and lying in the bow.

ROAD RAT. CROSS CANVAS. Psychotropic BREAKDOWN. An angel sent from heaven. Goddess pink and beautiful.

But I'm no angel. I'm no Joan of Arc. I'm no DOWN STREET DIRTY.

And I'm sorry for what I've done to myself. I fell in love with the devil inside of me.

FORGIVE ME NOW BLACK DEMON IN THE DEAD OF NIGHT.

Hark, Listen!

Hear my confessionals of word of what I exchange with you in a sleuth of red sauce and comforting please. Crazed elephants come palmy rotary-farms of cryogenic. Transgressions of jazz in alto sax. Sublime fountains of yellow clay-fish in an art-mix of flour, chips, cookies of raw pins, beat tunes, clowns not-yet-time sold baron of state. Hungry misers, fools passing plates, humiliations, fort tiaras pale, confectionery sweet, complementary cross limbs, strife three-ass tile, Tom Boujo's Atlanta, relief maps of sole platters, cry-gene kick stopped triangular confusion and placement of words, sentence in poem left by antecedent stew, broths of heat, word melt, decomposition, waste baskets, to be read by *no one*.

Declaration

Auspicious goglodites. Anomalous phantasms, cuntreation of the subliminal word melt. Freaky shlops of board and pieces, metallic rump.

Cancerous blob protrusion crying in the night: "I LOVE YOU. GOOD LORD I LOVE YOU." And the freaction pipéri somnambulism. Dreamy man-stands.

SOPRÉSA! MÁMMA!

Yuletides sang, calling queers of the earth to REVOLT the melt usurpers. Gonads scream: "IT IS TRUE!"

Quotidian jambles SHOVED into the generator. SHOVED into my suppository of pseudo-literature!

Human hosts boring into flesh so tender, oh so tender. And the animals: ants, worms, egrets coming in delight!

White cock! The bright dissimilitude of morning!

YOU HAVE NOTHING TO LOSE BUT YOUR LANGUAGE.

Word Melt

Fine-brine honey combed in fat clicks of chickens. Blood-blue pencils creamed psycho pottery. Black film of foreign beauty created, tightly blighted by bars of nymphic blots in jars of strawberry ice cream.

Come moralist pees of cups and come by on a pleated Borneo statuette. Combine lines to lime, aligned with yellow pox of green snot. Psychedelic culmination of Bob Dylan dyes of chromatic lip tripe, might?

Jungian symbols shaped like a phallic worm. Ascending staircases a conspiracy of main-screened Noula bums. White stirred mugs of browned leather. Picks protruding pavlovas of milk, the black piano keys.

Raped parchment of musty texts undone. Words slitted off propaganda posters printed in the psyche.

Oedipal kings, the coral moon. White pearly fluid dripping onto the car seat.

     Skeletal crayons.

     Beaten aged clams.

Pearls tipped in a cup of lumped pups. Paper inscriptions. Horror films synthesised into caddies' buried bottoms, an antecedent phrase.

Pun strobe light on a paid steak-rack. Juicy limp figs. Peristalsis of bum back bees.

Staging androids electrified into pale semen. Snowballs convulsed by machines into a disgusting melt.

Burly menstrual hairs, bleak and smoothed. Timbre of lilting bite.

Topika mushrooms tasty on margarine spreads. Butter slick coat of smitten cheese.

Cascading eyes down to a hole of clack emptiness.

Cry, cry, cry. Leave me by—and listen.

Genesis

Shouting and arguing. Bewildered and on edge. I race across the floorboards. Into the bathroom, the pill bottles lined up below the mirror. Shaking, the faucet bursts open and I take in mouthfuls of water.

Looking into the browny pits of my eyes. The gaze holds then collapses from view. Push forward into blackness.

<>

13 year old boy. Transferred following an intentional overdose of Flunitrazepam. Ingested 29 tablets. Went upstairs to the bathroom and came downstairs, appeared groggy and unsteady on his feet. Ambulance called. Empty bottle found in bathroom. Reports from toxicology incoming. Patient currently sleeping.

<>

Patient still sleeping. Should wake up from the effects of the drug in the morning. Should not need Flumazenil now.

End report.

Faggot Lucifer

The thought of it glowing inside me like a RED HOT fucking ember. Jesus please. Christ almighty. STRIKE. Our lady of Bordeaux, stab her in the spleen or morning tableaux. Calamitous friction. Tiled mosaic Islamic mirage, the shrink an anaemic purse of urine, concrete and SHIT. Coca-Cola Amatil. Faggot Lucifer. Five miles to Vegas in a pimp's car. "THE." Stop saying "the". "The" is the tyranny of the sentence. Three sees crap-o-thon Uncle Sam, baby of the racist pig Australia. Anabolic steroids of camouflage. The anal cavity needs examining, Mr. Verlaine. Top? Bottom? Versatile? Comatose? Pallid cuckoo bird of Octo-Ibis period, Egyptian pottery. Stigmatism. The doctor told me it was terminal, you stop-motion ballerina. St. Augustine, the rosary beads of pain. Acting is decay. For the beautiful ONLY. NO fags, jocks, nerds, liars, ANY, I repeat ANY, Oscar Wilde fanatics whatsoever. 101 days of sodomitical glory. King they call harem street. Gone are the sycophants, the liars, the stone-cold fucking CHEETAHS.

Stopping for a minute to examine my virgin. Jesus told me I could do anything I want. Even flog a beaten ice-worm Tupelo hoon.

I am a scholar of the highest. I am a scholar and nobody knows my name. But I am known to the Shrimp Honey Bunnies of Hollywood. Arrows in the Victorama carnival. Queen Victoria (she told me her name first) was a stop-road to the record factory in Brunswick. New Zealand and the Alabamy baby. Chaos was the first thing on my mind as his mind reached ANARCHY. Sweet, sweet shoreline. VISIONS. VISIONS. VISIONS. Fantastic visions of the exotica universe. Universe of eternal pain. Samuel had no child. Not a sinner in time for the ligature study of anything. Contortions on the carpet, I felt the sad low prod on my dick. Lover. Lover. Lover. Boo-hoo! No glue. No ideas whatsoever.

Septic Tank Universe

I live in a rectangle and it is the purity of the world in which I live. The sea surrounds the sun-silver walls which slithers radioactive junkie degenerates. Sklaaaaaatch, skraaaaaaaawww, shhhhhhhhhhlaaap of the tearing and pouring of blood, flesh and lime cascading from blades.

BUZZZZZZZZZZZZZZ

The sun-silver walls SHOOT five metres to the sun of the kingdom.

Government instruments penetrate with see-rays and battle with blood cameras that spray psychoactive substances to diffuse and disorient the opponent.

"Tut-tut," I mutter. "A warthog-in-mud tactic."

Someone shouts from crisscross metallic megaphones.

Government vehicles stride the sky with beeps, blips and clicks permeating from slits in the high-beam lights. The council cleaners strip the Government Manufactured & Crafted 1905-vintage wallpaper that is pasted onto the firmament. Waste is compressed into structure-cubes cut in 2cm intervals.

The Dettol lake sucks up the dirt-germs sourced from a

constellation of abscesses held in various city hospitals. The three-amigo checkpoints filter the scum-particles held in the backseat of a vomit-car dropped into the Dettol lake.

Behind, moving electric benches support statues which secrete white blood cells magnified-physical 2000 times. Autoclaves line the edges of the horizon. Steam puff furtive.

"Steam the air and strip it bare, boys."

All drugs anti-cover the 5-metre perimeter of my bedroom. All anti-this and anti-that. Anti-histamines, anti-biotics, anti-septics and anti-psychotics. But I have no need for any of these, rolling as my brain does, no contaminants required nor sprayed mind/fur-altering microbes (they fill the shelves). It's all anti-life. But purity and sterility wash the hands that forsake the filth. Eyes in an evil (they pierce the mirror) to which I stare in Kafka horror. My body is completely encased.

I am becoming a germ.

Flesh to Feed Souls of the Dying

1

The old man stands silently on the coast of Gibraltar. Marine biologists congregate on coastal plains. Rebirthing salt concentrate diluted in ailments of oil. Hercules long gone with pillars of crystal-puff from steam ships.

BRING BACK THE SMOKING BULLET!

Guns drawn out of side sockets! Shiny magnesium bullets penetrate skin! Dumbfounded tourists annihilated in blood baths! Cowering on leather car seats like god-fearing nuns!

Stick a crucifix in his ear! Strangle him with a hijab! Shove a toy Buddha down his throat! Engrave the star of David on his chest with hot pokers!

The Faggot Lucifer a poster boy for the Rapture as he shouts:

"Bow down before Trump, Bush and Nixon. Bow down before the flame skimmers as they upturn the skin on your pink thighs. Bow down to the sacred golden carcass of tax. Bow down before Nixon as he rapes his way through Vietnam. Bow down before Hoover as he records conversations in female toilet blocks.

Bring them back I say!

Bring back the death!

Bring back the blood!

Bring back the crystalline sex cult!

Herald it in with a Wagnerian tune!

Bring it all back I say!"

2

Traversing the hellscape in an automobile. Reptiles meander under sinewy blue wires of forest. Passing hybrid vehicles meshed with organic breathing steel. Government advertisements dispersed along the road, endorsing unsafe sex, smoking, drink-driving and outback murder. I gesture at hitchhikers on the roadside, tinkering with exquisite ballerina dolls.

A human carcass conversing with a prostitute, a cigarette clenched between stark, white enamel, a torn upper lip, a gouged eye and a protruding cheek bone.

Upright amphibians building shanty towns at Chernobyl. Cinema palaces attended by resurrected corpses wearing

3D glasses. Doling out human birth fluid in packages of detergent. Atheist lasagne prepared by Catholic priests. Abraham living in a makeshift tent with his three pimp wives, weeping tears of blood, soaking the parched highway of dissolution. The plundered land of the conquistadors. The revived cult of Cochimetl on Wall Street. The land where Fox News rigs the elections. Where pigsty billionaires run for president. Where movie stars scull their $99 protein pills prescribed by faux doctors that peddle heroin to make a living. Where Christian bigots regurgitate garbage to a crowd that listens. Where presidents cheat on their virgin wives. Where the leader with lips like an anus uses his dummy façade to reinstate the constitution of fortified garbage.

Don't listen to them: aberrations of the spirit, sociopaths of the soul—garrisons of the ego. The attar of the weeping ghost. "Don't listen to them," the patriots of the libido will tell you. They will tell you what to say and when to say it. But you are superlative in wisdom. You will not receive their compacted waste formations. Send it away, send it to the land of the cross and the phallus. The land of crying and shouting. The land of the begotten magpies. The land that is a Bosch painting. The land that is hell behind the smiling white man. The land that is truly hell.

Welcome to the land of decay. The land of the neo-Nazi and the KKK. This is the land of fear and paranoia. Of skylarking blood beasts. Victims of nuclear fallout hold their deformed babies with tongs. Cries of searing pain dissipate the soundscape of imminent death. Fresh flesh to feed souls of the dying. White cerebral pain of the land. The putrefaction of raping conquistadors and Aztec codices. Exiles and broken-down creatures line the tarmac like the poor in a soup kitchen. But there is no soup.

3

We're onto country now, the sweeping terrain of barley and corn. The plateau of corpulent baby tomatoes. The acerbic valley of the honeysuckle and the melted butter-yellow of the foxglove.

We passed the old man long ago and are onto different parts now, where the snot-green reptiles meander and the pudgy white worms of Christmas frolic on the crispy sand. Where the incessant drool of electric hiss and spark penetrates the ears and bursts the eardrums into a tarn of pus and red.

Yes, I saw it all en route through the asphalt jungle to the broken-down stars emanating puffs of petrol smoke, x-rays, gamma bursts and spectral light filaments convening at a point.

I saw the supersonic cafeterias automated with food production, packaging and distribution. I saw the reptiles building shanty towns at Chernobyl. I saw the church, abandoned by abuse. I saw the obscene light monster breaking the neon tubes off "JESUS SAVES" and flowing the chromatic gas onto its caecilian body as it descended from the steeple in a fine mist, eyes retreating into its sockets in an electro-phosphoric fix. Raw voltage spewing onto the side of the road like vomit.

Tax Fund Carcass

Keneally gibe way off track. New debt collectors to chase up fines. Councils declare war. O'Farrell's $5 fighting fund. Man flu leaves you cold. It's a feast of fish as shark pack leaps for lunch. Bracelet betrays a boozy actress. Car crash / turtle / man falling.

<>

He's daisy ducked with Rudd's tax carrot. Sour krauts at his tea party. Two more rebels. Bellamy feeling sorry for Israel. "Bite the bullet and embrace the body armour." Dorothy Wilkins, the day pulls out. Poetic revival a cabaret boost. First shot in air dog fight. Cheats plague casino. Twin brothers in suicide pact. Picasso takes tumble on muse. Work act worries. Clarke, Lara deal. What there is, was.

<>

A warning by ASIO on super tax. Teen faces drug charges. Mamma lass loses weight and finds wings. Let them taste travel troubles! Abduction alerts. Potatoes Protect. Downing tools. Whale alarm for the Japanese. Tragedy in Peru. Tripping life the monastic way, or how to enjoy being railroaded. Fears of double dip shackle the market. Another super tax? Supermassive death rebels. Recycled plans. No infrastructure. Public yet, maybe. The Northwest misses out.

<>

Going exploring. Troop truck inferno. Taliban gunmen destroy NATO convoy, killing seven. Chorus the reporters. "Yes," said Brumby. "What there is, was."

Coins

my fingers are as mean as worms

The Apotheosis of Hedwig Wilms at Berlin Buch

Diagnosis: Dementia praecox

She doesn't eat anymore. Force-fed by nasogastric tube.

1/8/1914	=	43 kg
15/8/1914	=	42.4 kg
1/9/1914	=	40.5 kg
13/9/1914	=	40 kg
1/10/1914	=	40.3 kg
15/10/1914	=	39.5 kg
1/11/1914	=	41 kg
15/11/1914	=	38.7 kg

Eats again. Constant weight loss.

1/12/1914	=	38.5 kg
2/1/1915	=	38 kg
1/2/1915	=	36.5 kg

Must be fed often with probe. Whines and cries a lot.

1/3/1915	=	33 kg
1/4/1915	=	31.5 kg
1/5/1915	=	33 kg
1/6/1915	=	32 kg

Generally quieter. Emaciated.

Does not take her prescribed medicine.

    1/7/1915   =   32 kg
    1/8/1915   =   29 kg

Patient continues to decrease in strength, weak and decrepit.

Collapses in the morning without regaining consciousness, dies at noon on 10/8/1915.

———————————————————————

"—the rapacious doctor cunts at Berlin Buch
                      were nothing but scoundrels—"

She tears her shirt. Nothing is clean. Ties the pillowcase around her neck.

Throws the bed on the floor.

HANG THE BLANKET FROM IT!

Babushka

The house was cold, like a wind had come in through the front door and stayed there.

I crawled down the corridor (Turkish hall runner beneath me) and knocked on the door where my grandmother slept. No answer.

I reached for the door handle, turned it and tottered inside. There she was—a torpid, veiny form sprawled out on the bed.

Her arms were covered with injection bruises that looked like watercolour droplets.

"Little Misha, little Misha, where are you?"

She had been blind for over 30 years.

Up on the bedside table—a black plasticky unit that played the local AM radio. Chanting music (always on Sundays) and crispy-thin voices penetrating through the static.

"Misha, Misha, are you there?"

I crawled back out the door.

She made me aware from a very young age that the body was a site of suffering.

Just the thought of it. There on the bed, for so many years.

Jacob's Dream

Fending off a tempestuous monsoon in Bali to protect my lodgings. A house well-furnished with Southeast Asian art, instruments and plants.

<>

Waiting on a train platform and continually catching the wrong one. Watching passengers depart and move on. I am stuck in the peak-hour motions.

<>

Strange and ethereal sounds coming out of a derelict house. I open the front door to see a phantom orchestra. The instruments are constituted from the body parts of humans and animals.

<>

My mother makes cuts across my body, neck and face with a kitchen knife.

Scene where I am fucking a piece of meat that is shaped like a human asshole. It looks like a palm-sized cut of raw beef steak.

<>

Gothic sandstone archways lead into a drab department store. Customers take new clothes off the shelves, wear them and have sex in designated booths. I spot a skin-tight jumper and try it on. It is grey.

<>

My father is storming around the house shouting and saying very bizarre things. I try to call an ambulance but every time I press the phone keys they shift and blur. On the tiny LED screen are the letters QQQ.

Try Something New: Porn

Emerald Ash. Popeye Catalufa. Black Tetra, Flame Skimmer. Candy Clam and Loco Lobo. Margate French-runt, Margaret Frech-unt. Margaret Fresh-hunt. Black Cherry Chalice. Mason Bee. Mr. Buck Moth. The Hawaiian Feather Duster. The green reptiles talk about me like a psychiatric patient. They study what he writes on the wall. "The product of a depraved mind," so they say. Walk side Wild. I'm the sick bitch!

Natural Causes

You are slowly dying.

Feel at peace with your internals turning into a mushy, black-bile goo as the virus eats its way out from the inside. Your finger-joints are snapping. The sheets are soaked in blood. The cleaner is not here until tomorrow. Imagine if she finds you on the bed like this—a puddle of fleshy swirls and ice-cream twists, the bones sticking out.

As the body goes, the mind too goes with it. You are trapped in a state of inertia. Try to stand up. The limbs are feeling loose now. You grab onto the curtains. But don't go too close to the window! The sunlight could speed up the decay. Your condition might scare the neighbours next door, and their sour cat.

Look around the room. It's nice, isn't it? Don't worry about the drawers full of notes. They will be here long after you are gone. And yes, your nail clippings will be donated to the Museum of Natural History. They will be catalogued, indexed and annotated by the head curator of preserved human anatomy.

Your name will live on. Your nails will live on. But you are here. Your eyes have popped out of their sockets. The carpet is splattered with intestines. Your thesis sits neatly up on your desk.

Your lips murmur as they are swallowed up by a pool of fleshy goo on the floor.

1453 A.D.

Pondering a flesh-filled hag of a decaying, miserable corpse. Slimy crackling turds and anxious meat ruckets, heeling on a cart of entrails dragged through the village square. Sagging skin-flaps drooping from eyeholes. Aimless, mindless, human meat. Preposterous, barely existing. Pawns in our little theatre.

Fagia

Food is detestable and spiritually impure, mouths slavered with saliva, crunching up sour pork belly, soda-fountain pancakes with gritty salt-clunks, garlic cloves lathered in chocolate puree.

The whole earth eating and excreting.

Garbage dumps and green slime oozing out the clamps: streaking stale milk, dog diarrhoea, alcohol vomit and sliming fruit juice.

And after this shit settles in your stomach, it lacerates your bowels with acids and stink and rot all through the small intestine.

Gobbly goop candies plastered to the sidewalk smeared with dog shit.

I wish I did not have to live on such a foul and degrading substance. Only serving to sustain this sagging piece of alien biology that is the body. Desecrating the soul with all that is the temporal and forbidden.

How awful to be trapped in this stinking, festering, vessel-filled pockmark. How can anyone be expected to rise above their mammalian condition and seek higher ideals with this deadweight? What a joke. I want out.

There is no other escape route except through all-out asceticism—depriving the body of nutrition for as long as possible until the soul tears through the flesh.

The path is clear. Exit body. Exit suffering. I abhor anything that is at the mercy of this most detestable of anatomies. Humans of the earth unite and be free of the decaying pisspot that is the human body.

Hedwig Wilms Redux

Parents both dead.   Protestant

seamstress   unmarried

heard voices   became dizzy

saw figures   relatives had beaten her

when asked who,   did not say

feels sick   suffers from melancholy

answers in a sad tone   patient discharged

transferred to   lunatic asylum.

People are following her   poisoning her

menstrual psychosis   last menstruation

two weeks ago   she has been beaten

to DEATH   eight days in bed.

Anaemic child   felt faint

sudden attacks   of vertigo

entering	closed rooms
strangely happy	believes her sister is ill
wants to be released	very calm
a little anxious	was fearful
and screaming	not able to be calmed
down,	fainting at work.
Patient lies in bed all day	was restless last night
distributes food	in the hall
not eating well	tore shirt
hid under covers	NOTHING CLEAN.
Quieter	emaciated
not talking	weak, decrepit
kicked the nurse	memory diminished.
Headache	fever

head heavy	NOTHING CLEAN
did not sleep	refused to eat
cleared out bed	banged on door
squats on floor	cries loudly
drums against windows	pinches lips tightly
lies down on floor	carried out screaming in the
highest tones	throws off pillowcase
has not slept all night	makes a grimace.

WASH YOUR NIGHT JACKET IN THE TOILET

Rubs thread from slippers	figures next to each other
sitting with a majestic air	refusing interference
yes/no	responses.
Transferred to	Berlin Buch

Psychiatric   Hospital.

Does not eat anymore   force fed with

nasogastric tube   busy again with crafts

eats again   constant weight loss

must be fed with probe   whines and cries.

* 29 kg*

EXITUS   LETALIS

collapses   in morning

does not regain   consciousness

dies at noon   August 10, 1915.

The Holy City

Starving, emaciated and completely insane.

I am dragged out of the house in the early hours of morning. The sun bright and flaming. Clutching an icon of Jesus Christ and praying for salvation.

All night long phoning emergency services, pleading with them for an urgent liver biopsy. My liver was turning to rot and I had little time left.

I had neither taken communion nor confessed in the past week, which meant I was destined for the pits of hell.

I remember the Jewish boy on the ward and the corned-beef dinners. And how long it took me to gain strength to walk.

On a hospital bed. A feeding tube pumping sustenance into my body. Sedate and lithe. Hums and beeps.

The Jamaican nurse sang me a gospel hymn after I showed her my religious bracelet.

I pieced through my meal to the verses of "Holy, Holy, Holy..."

Night of Glass

Grand piano ragtime farce. I am chased around an ivory-black piano with a belt. Like a bull: menacing, threatening. He cracks the whip on the hard tiles. I shriek as I avoid the striking strap. Mother and Sister sit in the lounge room, glued to the evening news, unfazed.

I play the ragtime psychotic duet, scrambling around the keyboard. His face red and enraged. Without asking for it. Fuming eyes. CRACK. I bolt to the front door and run out onto the streets screaming. Barefoot and wearing ripped pyjamas.

Tuning into static frequencies while I wander the dreamscape suburbia. Lights from windows and porches at every turn. The moon barely full, but the light bathes everything in an unreal glow.

I roam at night like a vampire. Cats hiss at me from under parked cars. Noises linger off the main highway, but here it is still and empty. Bloody and outcast, this vampire hovers towards the hubbub of cars. Towards civilisation— the bastion of steel, smoke, guts and madness. Past worn down houses, weeds and grasses spilling over the fence in the milky light of luna.

A bunch of garlic cloves hanging over the doorway. The

locals must have been informed of my undead wanderings. Alerts have been sounded and now a vigilante party is out to draw a stake into this monster's heart. Battery powered torches and gardening rakes for pitchforks. Garlic cloves placed atop every door to ward off this unwelcome evil. Crosses mar the footpaths.

Closer to the highway now. In an alleyway with garage-doors lining both sides. The rear ends of family homes and the resting place of garbage bins.

Smashed beer bottles glimmer under neon lights.

Little puddles of water filling up pits and cracks in tar.

Trees obscure the hazy view ahead.

Tiptoeing over luminous shards. Just beyond the ferns—a car pulls up beside the kerb. I am grabbed by the wrist and shoved into the backseat.

Live at the Whisky a Go Go

The billboards are up. Misha the Maniac plays live at the Whisky a Go Go. Watch him upturn seats. Slap his ass in leering fury. Raising his voice in ecstasy now, giving the middle finger to all the filth and corruption that consummates the earth. The punk band wrestles in the background as he screams all over the dance floor, writhing and squirming like an animal in the throes of death.

"Look at these jerks," Misha thinks, as he bays for his own blood, cutting his chest a cross-stitch with the house kitchen knives.

"YOU WANT BLOOD?" he shouts, wiping the sweat off his forehead.

"THERE WILL BE BLOOD!"

The band thrashes raggedly as Misha shoots his hand up in the air:

"STOP FOR FUCK'S SAKE, STOP THE MUSIC!"

But the band plays on. Snarling in disgust, this freak convulses across the stage in the raw heat of the music. "When I was five years old my mummy said to me..."

He trails off and glares at the audience, shoulders hunched

like a maniacal bull riding the frenetic drum stomping. Misha is unzipping his black leather pants, revealing leopard-print briefs.

Spitting everywhere he shakes the rags off his boots. The last drum roll sounds as the band catapults into the next number.

"Shove ya meat pies down ya filthy ass cracks!"

All sorts of crap is being thrown on stage. The lights bathe him in an array of sickening colours. The blood on his chest turns black, purple, then blue. Misha is swept up in the tides of history, his body torn asunder, exploding through the Whisky a Go Go. The guitars whine out.

Dodecameron Suite

1

As I went back to sleep around 7.45 am I dreamed that I was crawling on the ground with my forearms.

I was in the backyard of a coastal residence with a field of grass leading towards the edge of a cliff.

As I laid down on the grass I looked at a set of playing cards in my hands. I turned the cards over. They had drawings of William S. Burroughs on them in the manner of a playing deck. Burroughs was king, queen, jack and joker.

Suddenly, the weather changed from a cool breeze to a violent storm. From my position on the ground I tilted my head upwards and looked out beyond the cliff and into the horizon. I saw a bolt of lightning flash across the sky. The sound of the thunderbolt woke me up.

2

Fire apocalypse in the distance. Gargoyles, demons, monsters and troglodytes. They are coming towards us. It is inevitable, it is futile.

In the lounge room at home with my mother and father. It is night. Columns of red-hot flames burst upwards on the horizon.

Father is carrying on as usual: threatening, swearing and miserable. We are all about to be wiped out by the flames and monsters. How pathetic to be going on like this, in our house, our home, our last moments.

Knowing that we are all going to die, and that I can't stand my father's filth any longer, I pick up a wine bottle and bash the base of it into his face until it caves in. Father is finally dead. I can now spend my final moments in peace.

In the upstairs window of my neighbour's house I see Bob Dylan illuminated by a pale, yellow light. He is writing the lyrics for *Blood On The Tracks*. He doesn't seem fazed. I shut the blinds on Bob, turn out the lights and wait for the apocalypse to consume us.

3

Lying asleep in my childhood bedroom. The afternoon sun spreads a warm white on the baby-blue walls.

I open my eyes and see a man with long, shoulder-length hair rummaging through my wardrobe and trying on shirts. The man points to the clothes on the floor beside my bed and claims that they are his. I respond sternly and tell him to get out, while stressing that the clothes belong to *me*. The man leaves without argument and shuts the door behind him.

Time passes and I open my eyes again to see my mother standing in the doorway. She has come to collect my washing. At first she is still, but with subsequent gestures—like strokes of a paintbrush—she transforms into a Matisse nude, coloured in Fauveish reds, blues and yellows.

4

Confined to a mental institution. In my large, private room there is a projector and I watch films to pass the time.

I embody a female movie character who walks out of a subway. She buys a kebab from one of the stalls in an underground passageway. The proprietor prepares a special green meat that contains a stimulant similar to caffeine.

5

Embroiled in a conspiracy with a board of CEOs managing a renowned book publishing corporation. I find myself in the middle of an urban jungle with tall concrete towers bearing alien inscriptions.

Assuming the disguise of a company worker, I take a lift up to one of the levels to meet with the CEO.

I enter a small office space and see workers crowding around a computer screen. They are hacking into databases, seeking my personal information. I walk past, but they remain unaware of my disguise.

6

I am led towards the door of a grand, old mansion. I walk inside and am confronted with bizarre contraptions, creatures and annexes.

I manage to foil my conspirators and convince the creatures to take my side. I crawl through tight compartments, through bathrooms and kitchens, opening all the faucets in sinks and baths. The house begins to flood and I make my escape.

I am driving around the city with my sister and mother and it is raining heavily. The roads are flooding.

Back in the mansion with its endless chambers. I am watching a film about the house.

I also participate in the making of a film and am informed that it is an adaptation of a J.G. Ballard novel.

7

I am held hostage in a theatre by an insane matriarchal figure. The evil woman, whom I never see directly, mutilates a pregnant woman and takes out her placenta.

We are all taken to the "listening room", which resembles a well-furnished recording studio. The unborn baby's body is splayed out inside a rectangular glass vitrine. The body is part of an intricate audio amplification system. The sound is amplified through the corpse across fleshy blood-vessels that function as speaker wires, which are tied down on either side of the vitrine, so that the body is suspended in a Christ-like position.

A white and bespectacled middle-aged man demonstrates the system, and we are all forced to watch. I transform into a little girl and crawl under the blood wires without anyone noticing.

The man turns on a switch inside the blood-vessel amplifier box within the vitrine.

Sound bursts forth—powerful, clear and deafening. We are all amazed. The man tells us that he can play vinyl records on this contraption as he pulls out a David Bowie LP.

Sitting beside me is another hostage. He turns to me and we both embrace. I feel an overwhelming sense of love amidst this horrific scene.

8

My mother, sister and I find a cylindrical container on the bedside table in one of the rooms of our house. We peer inside and see a long, pink form floating on the water. It is encased in a condom filled with bloody fluid.

Small organisms begin to emerge from it, swimming around like sea monkeys. My sister tries to touch them, but my mother and I grab her by the wrists and warn her that they might be contagious.

The creatures grow until they spill out over the container. They take on pseudo-human forms with black, beady eyes. The creatures stick to each other—pink, swelling, slimy and bulbous—filling the entire room.

My father storms in and thrashes at the monstrous forms, but he is engulfed as they keep growing. The rest of us flee from the room and escape before the creatures destroy the house.

9

On a large passenger ship that resembles the Titanic. While on deck, I have a premonition that the vessel will crash and sink. I desperately try to find a way of disembarking before the approaching cataclysm.

The ship makes an unexpected stop at a port in order to let off sick passengers. Only a handful of people are allowed to disembark. I am the last person allowed to leave.

Once I arrive in the port, malicious unseen forces conspire to have me killed for escaping my fate on the ship. I furiously scramble around the city-port, jumping over fences, running through backyards and alleyways to avoid detection and capture.

10

From suburban streets I enter the grounds of a Victorian-era mansion.

The main complex houses a large library. As I scour the shelves, I come across a volume on Greek folk songs. The first part contains an anthology of lyrics. The second part an analysis and history of the verses.

The third is a CD with sound recordings of songs documented in the first part.

I try to borrow the book but the library closes. A sour-faced police officer waits for me in the reception area. We argue for a moment until an octopus appears and throws itself onto her face. There is much flailing, and the demonic octopus kills her.

I escape and make my way through the gardens, which have now swollen into a pond. As I shut the iron gates, I see the octopus behind me, submerging in the muddy water.

11

Conducting research in a New York City archive. I am looking through old photos of Greek and Māori musicians. The research library morphs into a ship which houses several collections—medieval armoury, rare books, photographs and Ancient Egyptian busts. The ship crashes and objects fly everywhere.

I hide a few valuable photos inside the pages of a dusty tome and hold it to my chest. In order to save the collections and crew we are transported back in time. To avoid detection, a crew member fashions cardboard models of subways and passengers in an underground bunker.

I escape with my female assistant through a subterranean elevator and emerge in a 16th-century Venetian port-city. I double as a Greek merchant from the island of Kefalonia. I communicate to others in English although I speak with a Greek accent. We visit an antique store run by pirates. To our horror they are salvaging treasures from our wrecked ship. I ask the proprietor if he has any photographs for sale (it is now the 19th-century and cameras exist) and the pirate snarls at us.

Demonic green warrior creatures storm this dimension unannounced and slaughter the city's inhabitants. An intergalactic agent who has full diplomatic immunity recognises my importance and protects me from the creatures by sealing me (and my assistant) in a plastic-coated sac of electric blue fluid. My leg tingles and spasms with currents.

The city morphs into an ancient Atlantis-like isle with temples, statues, baths, gardens and terraces. A vessel appears in the sky with two holes in it, from which water gushes forth.

The island is flooded and earthquakes rock the earth. The city-isle is engulfed by tsunamis. My assistant and I morph into water gods and lie in wait on the shores of an opposite isle. A tsunami approaches us and I use my force to halt the waves, which fly upwards and over us—behind the isle's colossal stone arch and mountain tops.

On reporting back to apocalypse headquarters, I am informed that the warrior creatures had no authority to destroy the dimension we were in.

12

An old coffee house in Athens or Piraeus in the early 1900s. Tough guys and hoodlums are seated around tables, smoking and playing dice.

As I make my way deeper into the cafe, I hear a haunting and melancholy jazz tune. Nobody notices my presence, so I decide to take flight and float above the customers.

Like a heralding angel I announce in Greek: "Forever free, Greece will be!" Everyone looks up from their tables and bursts into laughter.

Embarrassed, I fly into the bathroom and try to escape through the toilet window. I smash the glass with my elbow but still can't fit through the opening. I fly back into the cafe to find it deserted.

As I descend to the ground it transforms into an old dance hall, then into the lobby of a bland, modern hotel. I feel a sense of loss and nostalgia for the old, lively characters back in the cafe. I walk out through the revolving doors.

Polka-dot

Think of poor Sylvia Plath
gassing herself to death
in a squat London flat

or the pigeons which just
took flight off the gutter.

This Could Be Anywhere

Joe McCarthy has been dead for over a hundred years, yet he is more alive than anybody. He assumes a pharaonic stance on billboards lining the packed freeway. The rain beats on car windows, and a promotion on toilet paper pierces through the static. I look ahead, and through the exhaust fumes are figures in police uniforms. It's a horrible sight; faces bleeding and bodies lying on compacted metal. There is only one car on the scene, and I'm sure this is a rigged crash. The police are always orchestrating building collapses, infectious outbreaks and automobile accidents. I drive off, straining to think of where I heard of this theory.

<>

Wandering lights stream through the shades like a carnival. But no one is out there, except the drunken policemen. I hear their vans skidding around a kerb while I swallow pills with sour juice. I switch on the television, ensuring that the volume is low, but the reporters whine above all consciousness and thought.

There is no comfort in any of this. Not the stale cheeseburger in the fridge, the gunshots outside or the droning television. Sedation sets in quickly and with flow. It dulls my senses and then branches out like veins all over my body. I stumble towards the couch and fall into its embrace. One of the springs is broken.

The visage of Ann comes into view as I fumble around for the remote. I change channels and a Coca-Cola commercial blares on-screen. I turn it off and watch the police make their rounds outside.

Konzert

Sound clear and deafening. Total amplification.

<>

The master of proceedings cuts himself repeatedly.

<>

Bouzoúki / baglamás / tzourás: essential instruments
of the lumpenproletariat.

<>

Visions through trained mediums.
Tobacco and pieces of cake. Libido of fish.
Ransacking the taverns.

<>

I don't know what love is but it's choking my oesophagus.

<>

Vacuum cleaners / sleeping bags / a cassette tape
of wailing laments.

The fascist bulimic monster enters.
Pasolini lives and his killers will be annihilated.

<>

Silver foil covering the floor / pink drapes
on the wall. Kitchen-sink language.

<>

Madness isn't just something to write about
in books. It's the spitting of bile / mental wards /
near misses / lonely agony / and hardly ever literary greatness.

<>

You must have no qualms about making a fool
of yourself in front of friends / colleagues / lovers.

<>

The speaker rants and foams at the mouth / vomits.

EXEUNT AUDIENCE.

Static Bugs

The artist's face was poised and still, his swirling blue eyes fixed on the horizon. He turned towards the canvas, and then to me, with a distressed look.

"I don't feel like painting, I just want to sit down."

A water-orb materialised in front of him as he sat down on the cane chair. His neck creaked and spat in spontaneous mechanical jerks. Cockroaches lurked deceptively inside cracks on the concrete-plastered walls.

The artist whistled a pleasant melody as the heel of his shiny leather boot twisted in sideways spasms on a chestnut cockroach. He strolled towards a box full of junk and picked up a cookie jar decorated with Chinese dolls. He dropped the insect inside, poured in some turpentine and set it alight. He placed the flaming jar on a pedestal. Cries of pain and nerves singed in acid.

It was dark outside and the flames fizzled in and out of being as the walls were illuminated by bursting streaks of light.

The view through the window was beautiful. The moon revolved in circles as the desert terrain was milked by its rays. The stars frolicked on the ledge as needles of light penetrated a vase of trodden flowers.

A wolf wailed as fifty-metre knives erupted from the sand. They pierced the moon while multi-eyed creatures masqueraded in pagan processions. Flash, rattle, circle, scream, convulse, worship, hawk, spasm.

<>

Somewhere in the artist's studio on December 17, 1914. Proclamations out of the radio and a man in a thick stringy voice:

"My static bug is black, about the size of a microwave and is native to CBS News but the law knows nothing about it... ha...ha...ha."

The static bug agreed in impure laughter.

The sun rising, a desert haze. Two kangaroos copulating with an eagle behind a dead cactus on which sat two koalas with bleeding tumours on their faces. How peculiar, and I thought this was Australia. The artist was applying the final strokes to his magnum opus, comforted by the static bug's tight, subversive radio-waves.

I lit a cigar and the flame licked the wrapper as it blackened and smouldered onto the carpet. A small trinket of flame pooled on the edge and swelled. The artist collapsed and asphyxiated with his hands cupped against his mouth, screaming rape through his atrophied eyes.

One look at the canvas affirmed my belief that the artist was a pretentious idiot. Blobs of agglomerated paint oozed off the easel. I strolled through the crackling fire and left, hearing it spit, "Mmmmm, that's some tasty art."

I watched as it catabolised the house in hunger, fuelled by the damp stench of turpentine and blood. The static bug scurried in insect-distress out of a gaping hole in the roof. It hissed in spasmodic electro-fluidic breakdown, its dying words:

"There's nothing here, we'd better move on..."

N.D.E. convulsions from a dying sage.

Smoke rose to the firmament as a man drove by in a Cadillac.

His head was on fire.

Event Scores

They took me to see a witch doctor because they thought I was possessed. The old woman performed a ritual with holy water, oil and a chalice. She anointed my head, prayed and watched the oil inside the cup; floating, congealing.

<>

I can feel cockroaches crawling all over my body. I can't sleep. My entire body infested with bugs crawling on my skin.

I take a pair of craft scissors and start scraping my leg with them.

<>

"Hold him down!" she yells, as she holds her palms against my face—"I can see it in his eyes!" My wrists have bruises all over from being restrained.

The security guard shoves my arm behind my back and I cry out in pain.

"Your chicken bone arms," he laughs.

<>

I secretly strike matches while nobody is around.

Bewildered by the flaming tip.

I light matches and drop them into every garbage bin I pass, closing them behind me.

<>

I carve notches into my wooden bedside table. Scrawling in red pen on the pages of my school notebook: "Peter is a sex slave in secret, hiding." I tear off the fragment and place it under my pillow. From my speaker plays the Talking Heads song "Burning Down The House".

I strike a match and drop it onto my pillow.

The fabric quickly catches fire.

<>

My finger is bleeding because I have picked at it.

I hold up a knife because my family is trying to kill me.

Holy God, Holy Mighty, Holy Immortal, have mercy on us.

<>

I walk all the way back to school to retrieve my books. It is closed, but I start climbing the fence. Someone shouts at me from a car that has pulled up beside the kerb.

<>

My parents have hired a hitman to murder me. I barricade my bedroom door to prevent any assassin from entering. Furiously scrawling on a scrap piece of paper:

SEND HELP. MY PARENTS HAVE HIRED A HITMAN TO KILL ME. IF YOU FIND THIS LETTER I AM PROBABLY DEAD. CALL 000 AND PLEASE REPORT TO POLICE IMMEDIATELY.

<>

I write out an SOS message in blue biro and fold it into the shape of an aeroplane. I throw it out the window.

<>

I try to escape through the bathroom window. I am held down, restrained and thrown into the back of a police wagon. "TAKE OFF YOUR BELT," the officer shouts.

<>

People are talking about me like I am a homosexual. Furtive whisperings. Means that they are in on my murder plot.

I lie down horizontally so that I can prevent my liver from failing.

People are talking about me on the television. I have spent the night secretly transcribing the nurses' conversations. The nurses are in on the whole thing.

<>

I punch her in the face and her nose starts bleeding. Someone enters and shouts: "What have you done?"

<>

This hospital admission was nothing but a game, a moral test. If I act correctly, I will be rewarded.

I am going on leave this afternoon, which means I will return home and my family will surprise me with a big celebration announcing the conclusion of this "test". There will be television crews and partying to welcome me back.

The End, My Friend

I took a bottle of pills and listened to The Doors to see me out.

Still conscious.

The walls adorned with posters of all the abstract masters.

I saw Jackson Pollock, alone in his studio. Hands smothered in enamel paint, the blank canvas stretched out before him, grandiose and redemptive.

Began to feel drowsy. Stashed away the plastic bottle as a woman entered. She took no notice as I stumbled through the door, down narrow, oppressive corridors. The office in sight. Shaking, eyes half-closed, slurring my speech.

Their faces began to turn. A wailing siren. A scurrying of feet. Lazarus, Jesus Christ, Archangel Gabriel and the Holy Ghost.

Help me.

Oil Blood Bones Stigmata

I swear that my body will be remade! It will be remade in the image of Our Lord Jesus Christ Our Saviour.

Blood, bones, thorns, flesh, stigmata, the whole fucking lot!

Corpus

my body is a constellation of aches

EAT THE WORDS

AND THE PEOPLE WILL EAT THE WORDS AND THEY WILL SLAY THEM AND MAKE LOVE TO THE WORDS AND THEY WILL MAKE LOVE TO THEM IN THE MOONLIGHT AND YOU WILL LOVE THEM FOREVER IN THE MOONLIGHT TOO AND THERE WAS A HARE AND THE HARE SPOKE AND HE GAVE EVERYTHING THAT HE COULD BECAUSE HE WAS A LOVELY HARE AND THE HARE LOVED ME AS IT LOVED YOU AND THE HARE CRIED AND CRIED AND IT LOVED TO CRY AND IT LOVED TO MAKE LOVE BEFORE SPRINGTIME BEFORE THE GREAT HUNTERS OF YORE SPRANG UPON THE VALLEY AND THE PEOPLE SAID THAT THEY WILL EAT THE WORDS AND MAKE A MEAL OF THEM FOR THE HARES TO EAT AND THE HARES WILL MAKE LOVE AGAIN AND AGAIN AND THE HARES WILL BE HAPPY

AND THEY WILL EAT THE WORDS
AGAIN AND AGAIN IN THE
MOONLIGHT AND I WILL LOVE
THEM AND I WILL SAY IT AGAIN
AND AGAIN IN THE MOONLIGHT
GOOD GOD I LOVE YOU AND
THESE GODFORSAKEN HARES
AND THEIR LOVERS AND THEIR
WIVES FAR OUT INTO THE
DESERT THE HARES WILL GO
AND WE WILL LOVE THEM
JUST LIKE WE LOVED THEIR
FOREFATHERS AND THEY WILL
LOVE US AND THEY WILL LOVE
US UNTIL THEY DIE AT THE
HANDS OF THE HUNTER AND
THEY WILL EAT THE WORDS
AND THEY WILL EAT THE
HARES AND THERE WILL BE
BLOOD AND HAIR AND MEAT
TO EAT THE WORDS FROM THE
HARES AND WE WILL EAT THEM

JUST LIKE WE ATE THEIR BABIES AND THEIR YOUNG IN THE MOONLIGHT <u>GOD</u> THEY WILL SMITE US WHEN THEY RISE UP FROM OUR CHAMBER POTS AND EAT THEIR WORDS AND THEIR SHIT AND OUR FLESH GOOD GOD I WILL LOVE THEM AGAIN IN THE MOONLIGHT FOR THE LONELY WILL NEVER GROW OLD WITH THEIR HARES AND THEIR YOUNG AND THEIR LOVERS AND THEIR FLESH AND THEIR SHIT IN THE MOONLIGHT AND THEY SHALL REMAIN HAPPY WHILE THEY EAT THEIR WORDS AND THEIR BABIES JUST LIKE THEIR MOTHER SAID AND WE WILL BE HAPPY AND WE WILL LOVE EACH OTHER AGAIN AND AGAIN AND AGAIN IN THE MOONLIGHT.

Jump Cut

You've smashed through an all-time low and it keeps getting lower, until your bladder moulds into your head and your legs descend like tentacles, your face an agaric infection. Spots and blisters bursting from soggy pores.

Spongy tainted cheese whiffs a stink of rot. Razor blades on my fingers. Razor blades on my knees. A double helix pattern slashed across my wrist, a typewriter and a rocking horse.

Dream Places

           Parking lots

                                tunnels

stairwells   footpaths

                highways

                                drains

                      skyscrapers

supermarkets

                                libraries

        clinics

                        smoke-stacks

                sewers

---

pools   oceans

        harbours

                      crystals

  canyons   cliffs   ravines

                    geysers

Dachau Blues

I feel the weight of history under my eyelids. I can see the stains of exile and genocide on my teeth. The cavities are death-pits. Bodies are thrown in until my breath becomes stale and rancid—teeth acid yellow.

Fantasies, yearnings and dreams of all humankind concentrated into the black pearl—my pupil.

The only salvation or redemption one could hope for—

A couple of freckles around my cheekbone—

Death

Wood of Suicides

Leaves flaring like sinuses on fleshy stems. Mud stench. Spotlights on droopy sinus. Short stumps of trees, lopped-off fingers. Trash. Spiny bushes, browned and stiff. Bark shaved bare, bleeding. Stick-strewn spider web. The gentle crush of scooters and clickety-clack noises from bicycles. Leaves eaten away. Swampy fallout. Only the sounds of bikers in this barren, lifeless crop. Sun blinding me through dead trees. Web stretches from stick to bony stick. More trees lining the roads. Long weeds hanging down like hairy scalps. Smoke rising up through the canopies. Mangrove bunches by highways. Bike trails carved out by big, gritty bulldozers. Telephone towers thrust up like phalluses from sparse places in bush.

Death Piece

I cried and cried but no one came. I was hungry. I was dying. I had days to live. My hands were clasped and I prayed for salvation. I prayed and prayed until my knees were sore and bloody but no one came. My liver had turned to rot and I was going to HELL. I looked in the mirror and saw a lizard staring back. I had wasted away. I was dying, I had days to live. I was still praying and praying but the end didn't come. I was lying on a bed with tubes coming out of me. I was tired. I was scared. I tried to run and hide but it was too late. I heard everyone wishing me well. I thought I was going to die a slow and painful death. My liver had turned to rot. If I didn't pray now I would be dining in HELL with the torture machines and the gamelans of pain. Everyone had alien smiles and plastic food. Flowers did no good. All my friends had left and I was an alien. An ALIEN. Peace never came. I had sinned and it had all gone to SHIT.

Nausea

Worn down by years of abuses. Gross, torpid body, lying in a cake of piss, blood, scabs and swollen appendages. Gross vile bile swirling in a mess of opiates and anti-psychotics. Coked up chocolate coursing through the swollen intestines, gaseous tripe. Soon the sugar shall sear my insides, filling my head with acid juices—germs and viruses extorting the little grey matter that I have left. Let me be squashed like an insect on this Persian rug, green gook slobbering over the sides of my twitching cockroach legs. Bloated belly from the ten thousandth meal of gorge. Doughnut crumbs, leftover caramel, now a purple-green, drops smeared over in sickly floral patterns. Shlop of ratty burps. Conning the last meal out of here.

Scratchy and endlessly on the edge. My skin to scrape back and reveal the tiny lice swarming under the skin flaps of my right buttock. I've never felt so much sensitive skin, and stink and slimy over my hairy body. The teeth piss-yellow, crammed in-between the white blobs of excesses from all the chewy mushy bread and stale milk. My anus fired by the stink that preceded it. God help the poor suffering fool. With so many bodily organs, all competing for conscious attention to win the ultimate prize of the most nauseating bodily function. Pukey, swollen and bruised. Stuffed with brusque, hairy hands.

Discharge Summary

Presented in acutely psychotic	state
brought in via	ambulance
called ambulance over five	times
belief that organs were	failing
felt he was dying	due to organ failure
if he ate or drank	this would worsen
his condition	refusing oral intake
praying to an icon with	Jesus' image
could not be distracted	from doing so.
Preoccupied with inner sadness	sees food as
temptation of SATAN	praying for help
guilt	sinfulness
clinically cachectic	and dehydrated.
Spoke in soft, inaudible voice	moderate eye contact

flattened affect	very abnormal
thought	content
obsessive about icon of Jesus	preoccupied that
his organs were	failing
refusing to eat and	drink.
Denied auditory or	visual hallucinations
when praying was	unaware
of his surrounding	environment
not acknowledging	others
not answering	questions
restless	oversedated
agitated	aggressive.
Week prior to admission	exhibited disturbed
and anxious behaviour.	Left book at school

returned after hours to retrieve it	nihilistic delusions
to do with	fact
that he was going to	die
gave all his new things	to charity
asked his "last rites" to	be read out to him.
Feelings of guilt	around sin
stated he was praying	for forgiveness
when asked	what sins these were:
gluttony	sloth
and wrath.	Constantly reciting
prayers to icon,	stigmata of
protein calorie	malnutrition.
Described	attended
received	wanted.
Expressed confusion over	sexuality

had found "gay fantasy" written in his diary

had spoken to him about "hormone cure".

Needed to pray to have a connection with God.

PO4 **Mg** **LFT**

AST 62 **47** **ESR-3**

Organs disintegrating

socially withdrawn depressed

overdose of benzodiazepines

behaviour consistent with

prodromal psychosis

medication later ceased

anorexia vulnerability

psychosis malnutrition

claimed symptoms were fabricated

would scratch himself.

P450 **CT** **BRAIN**

EEG **DNaseB** **ASOT**

Cautiously cooperative   engageable

rehydration   intravenous fluids

oral   intake

fed via nasogastric   tube

involuntary patient   phosphate habit.

ALT 47 **Ca** **FBC**

Cytochrome **Folate** **Lipids**

[within normal limits]

[within normal limits]

[within normal limits]

[within normal limits]

                    [within normal limits]

               [within normal limits]

                    [within normal limits]

                    [within normal limits]

          [within normal limits]

                    [within normal limits]

                    [within normal limits]

     [within normal limits]

                         [within normal
limits]

                    [within normal limits]

          [within normal limits]

                         [within normal
limits] [within   normal limits]

               [within

                                    normal lim its]
                    [within norm al limits]
                        [with in normal
limits]   [within normal limits]
         [within   normal   limits]
                        [within
                normal
                    limits]   [with in
            limits] [within   normal limits] [within
norm al limits] [within   norm al   ]
   [within   limits] [with in   normal limits]
[within   no rmal limits] [within   normal limits]   [within
        limits]   [normal limits] [normal
    limits] [within   n or mal limit s] [within   no rmal   ]
                [within   limits] [within   normal
        limits]
[with   in   ] [within   no rmal lim its] [within
    no rmal limits] [within   no rmal limits] [within
            ] [within   normal   ] [within
nor mal lim its] [within   normal limits] [with   in   normal
limits] [within   normal limits] [within
                limits] [within
        lim its] [with   in
                    no   limits]   [within   normal
lim   its] [within   normal limits]
            [normal limits] [within   norm al limits] [within   no
rmal lim its] [within   normal limits]
                [within normal limits]
        [with in
                        norm al

The Puppet

Inspiritus sanctus

lapis lazi enterest

von greppen rart

le pupesse des lubenshraft

los spectatorast in lopus lazuli

fornalakia per la marmalakia

koolist kon koolish

invis, ivris aeter vosh loobenstat

sofrosini von greppen lart

lip lopassa dresht-lap oulira.

KRALIA—MOOPITAR—ASHITAR!

BEGON!

Notes

Extract from *Madness and Civilization* by Michel Foucault reprinted with permission from Taylor & Francis Informa UK Ltd - Books.

'The Apotheosis of Hedwig Wilms at Berlin Buch' & 'Hedwig Wilms Redux':

These texts are based on the original medical case notes of Hedwig Wilms, a patient and artist whose work is held in the Prinzhorn Collection & Museum in Heidelberg, Germany. The author has loosely translated and re-arranged entries in this case file with permission from the Prinzhorn.

This collection bears the name of Hans Prinzhorn (1886–1933), an art historian and psychiatrist, who by 1921 had amassed over 5,000 artworks created by patients in German-speaking mental asylums. The Prinzhorn Collection is still housed on the grounds of the Psychiatric Clinic at the University of Heidelberg, along with a permanent museum which changes its exhibition displays up to four times a year.

From the case file held by the Prinzhorn, we learn that Wilms was a seamstress by occupation, and that at the age of 38 she was admitted to a hospital in Berlin after she started to hear voices and suffer from fainting spells. Her condition was described in now-defunct diagnostic terms like "menstrual psychosis" and "hysterical mental disorder".

By the time she was admitted to the Berlin-Buch Psychiatric Hospital in July 1913, her condition had deteriorated, and she was summarily diagnosed with "dementia praecox". She was put on a meal plan and had to be force-fed with a nasogastric tube. Her weight data was recorded every two weeks in the margins of her case file. The final entry records her weight at 29 kg. Ten days later Wilms collapsed and never regained consciousness, dying at noon on August 10, 1915.

Today, Wilms' primary legacy rests in a sole surviving work that was donated to the Prinzhorn after her death. It consists of a serving tray with a jug and coffee pot crocheted from cotton yarn. The work has been widely exhibited and is an important precursor to the feminist soft sculptures of Méret Oppenheim and Yayoi Kusama.

Hedwig Wilms: "Tray with coffee pot, milk jug" (1913-1915).
Cotton yarn, macramé. Tray: 22.5 x 30.5 cm; coffee pot: height 16.5 cm, milk jug: height 4.5 cm. Inv. No.: 90, 91, 92.
© Prinzhorn Collection, University Hospital, Heidelberg.

'Discharge Summary'

This text is drawn from my personal psychiatric case notes. It is part of a larger documentation project I call the "psychotic archive", which involves collecting the documents, writings, artworks and objects connected to my experiences with madness.

To build this archive, I have requested copies of medical case notes, annotated drawings made in hospital, collected used medication packets, and reconstructed artefacts which were lost or destroyed. Some of the writings in this book were sourced from my initial confrontation with psychosis, dating back as far as 10 years. A few workbooks of writings and digital word documents from this period I destroyed shortly after out of shame.

Archiving these psychotic experiences has been a powerful act of restitution and sense-making. This process takes on a special importance when we consider that the mad have nearly always been narrated by psychiatry; their creations collected, annotated and curated by institutions and by people who have never experienced madness themselves.

To be mad is like a state of possession or bewitchment, a conjuring of entities and irrational forces. But rather than being the legacy of a curse, the texts presented in this book have instead become a source of power and affirmation.

A terrible sickness has followed me all my life, but these writings are a raucous proclamation of sanity against the forces that threatened to destroy me.

    I am only now starting to win back that power...

Biography:

Misha the Maniac is a nom de guerre and alter-ego. It was born out of the author's psychosis and is a means of vocalising the extreme mental states, thoughts and ideas central to that experience.

www.ingramcontent.com/pod-product-compliance
Lightning Source LLC
Chambersburg PA
CBHW030302010526
44107CB00053B/1785